THE BEST OF EAST LEICESTERSHIRE & RUTLAND

Leicestershire and Rutland divided into hundreds, showing the market towns (indicated by their own symbol), po stages and one borough town. This fascinating map was published in 1761 by W. Owen for the *General Magazine Arts and Sciences*. It was engraved by Emanuel Bowen and Benjamin Martin. Melton Mowbray, 'Okeham' a Uppingham are clearly shown.

THE BEST OF EAST LEICESTERSHIRE & RUTLAND

TREVOR HICKMAN

SUTTON PUBLISHING LIMITED

First published in the United Kingdom 2001 by
Sutton Publishing Limited, Phoenix Mill
Thrupp, Stroud, Gloucestershire, GL5 2BU

British Library Cataloguing in Publication Data
A catalogue record for this book is available from the British Library

ISBN 0-7509-2775-5

Title page photograph: Carnegie Library, 1910, now Melton Mowbray Museum.

Typeset in 10.5/13.5 Photina.
Typesetting and origination by
Sutton Publishing Limited.
Printed and bound in England by
J.H. Haynes & Co. Ltd, Sparkford.

By the same author:

Around Melton Mowbray in Old Photographs
East of Leicester in Old Photographs
Melton Mowbray in Old Photographs
The Melton Mowbray Album
The Vale of Belvoir in Old Photographs
The History of the Melton Mowbray Pork Pie
The History of Stilton Cheese
Melton Mowbray to Oakham
Around Rutland in Old Photographs
Leicestershire Memories

CONTENTS

Tourists   6

Introduction   7

1. Melton Mowbray   9

2. Melton Borough   37

3. Oakham   77

4. Rutland   103

    Bibliography   158

    Acknowledgements   159

    Selective Index   160

Tourists standing at the Market Cross in front of Thomas Cook, Melton Mowbray. The company was the first to promote tourism throughout the world. The visitors are the Grech family accompanied by friends from the island of Malta, who were in this historic market town as tourists. They were fascinated by the cattle market and the local produce on sale at stalls in the street. This method of selling goods and livestock has been a feature of Melton Mowbray for over 1,000 years. Standing, left to right: Connie, Stephen, Carl, Georgina, Chloe, Amy, Sharon and Vince. Sitting: James and Steve.

INTRODUCTION

In recent years much has been published concerning the character and history of East Leicestershire and Rutland. I have been involved in writing ten books that cover the history of this area, with particular reference to the three market towns of Melton Mowbray, Oakham and Uppingham, all steeped in history. In addition to compiling my own books, since 1963 I have given help and advice to other authors working on accounts of the area. Many of the books published with my involvement have been circulated throughout the world. They have created considerable interest in this part of England and have encouraged people from numerous countries to visit East Leicestershire and Rutland. I have been contacted personally concerning the content of books that I have written or assisted in publishing. Many casual visitors to the area have become friends, and they have come back again and again. Because of the nature of my interest in local history, we discussed my numerous books, but above all those who came wanted to see the historic places of interest in the area. Over many years I have compiled a list of sites in East Leicestershire and Rutland that I consider to be worth exploring and have shown them to visitors from the USA, Canada, Europe, Australia and New Zealand – and of course to many friends who come to these two counties from elsewhere in Great Britain and who consider the countryside in this area to be 'Forever England'.

In *The Best of East Leicestershire and Rutland* I have once again compiled a book on local history covering the area of England that has been my home for over sixty years. It could be considered a tourists' collection – certainly every feature, village, event and market town I list or mention in the pages that follow I have visited personally, in some cases many times. In every instance, family, friends, colleagues and visitors have joined me in viewing these places of interest. Occasionally, during visits I have organised for other people, I have been asked to compile a book based on the places on the itinerary. At last this is what I have done. It is my selection; I have not been involved with any organisation other than my publisher, who has given me support throughout its compilation.

Local history is the theme. I commence with a look at the market town of Melton Mowbray. The first pages of Chapter 1 cover the cattle market, which has operated in this small town for over 1,000 years, a fact confirmed by a deed engrossed in 1077 and held in the British Museum. Markets held in Oakham and Uppingham began at a similar time, although in these two towns the weekly cattle sales have now ceased. Recently farmers' markets have been launched in this locality. The first was held in

Melton Mowbray at the cattle market site off Scalford Road and now takes place every Friday. Similar events take place in the grounds of Oakham Castle and at Mercers Yard, Uppingham, also on Fridays. Street markets operate on various days, along with an antiques market in Melton Mowbray's market place on Wednesdays. Markets were the essential life blood of any agricultural area in days gone by, but now only occasionally do a few villages hold them. Exton in Rutland has a market on and around the village green in May each year; this is a village tradition and a taste of history.

The towns and villages of East Leicestershire and Rutland are steeped in the past. Without doubt the foremost historic site in the area is Belvoir Castle, which is always worth a visit, especially when special events are arranged, such as a medieval jousting tournament. Many features of the area are best viewed one after another – set aside a day, visit an historic site in the morning, then have lunch or refreshment at a superb local inn or visit an equally fine restaurant.

An aspect of life in this part of England that has generated much interest is the history of the development of Stilton cheese and the commercialisation of the Melton Mowbray pork pie. My Pork Pie and Stilton Trail, which will take a whole day for a visitor to complete, begins on page 50. Pork pies and Stilton cheese are the taste of this district, a must. Cheese was the mainstay of village businesses in the area from the middle of the eighteenth century to the turn of the twentieth when commercialisation transferred manufacture of the traditionally farm-produced cheese to factory-based dairies. On page 125 I record an historic achievement in the County of Rutland – the reintroduction of the famous slipcote cheese, which is produced in a small dairy at Lyddington. Up to the outbreak of the First World War this cheese was as famous as Stilton. At the turn of the twentieth century it was selected by connoisseurs of fine cheese to be served to MPs in the restaurant at the Houses of Parliament.

In order to appreciate what this part of the East Midlands has to offer, a visitor should stay a few days. Anyone contemplating coming to the area should contact the local tourist information centres; they hold an extensive range of leaflets and flyers covering most of the sites included in this book.

Most of the photographs, historic and modern, that are included in this book have never been published before. I hope the reader enjoys this collection and uses *The Best of East Leicestershire and Rutland* as inspiration to visit this area of England and enjoy so much that is the best of the East Midlands.

Trevor Hickman
January 2001

1

Melton Mowbray

Melton Mowbray is a medieval market town, the only one in Leicestershire to be listed in the Domesday survey as having the right to hold a market, which was granted in 1077. Trading in sheep was the main reason for the establishment of the market. In 1066 England was an important centre for the wool trade and exports to continental Europe generated enormous income. The Norman William the Conqueror was encouraged to invade Saxon England by the prospect of increasing his domination of European trade. Melton Mowbray's sheep market was situated on land indicated by the Sheep Cross, now called the Corn Cross, at the junction of High Street, Nottingham Street and Cheapside. The sheep trade still plays its part in the weekly sales held on a Tuesday at the cattle market off Scalford Road.

THE CATTLE MARKET

Melton Mowbray cattle market, 1906.

Sheep for sale at the weekly auction at the cattle market.

Locally raised pigs for sale at the cattle market. They might be converted into Melton Mowbray pork pies.

Farmers, visitors and tourists viewing one of the weekly auctions of cattle.

Storage sheds for cattle at the market, 1996.

Auctioneers at work selling young cattle in the ring, 1996.

A cow and a calf being sold by auction at the cattle market.

Cash is needed at a cattle market. These were the offices on site in 1996.

An antiques market is held off Scalford Road simultaneously with the Tuesday cattle market and is enjoyed by visitors to this area of town.

The sale by auction of poultry, rabbits and pets at the Tuesday Melton cattle market, 1990.

An early call 'rooster' from Melton Market.

Empty poultry pens.

MELTON: STREET MARKET

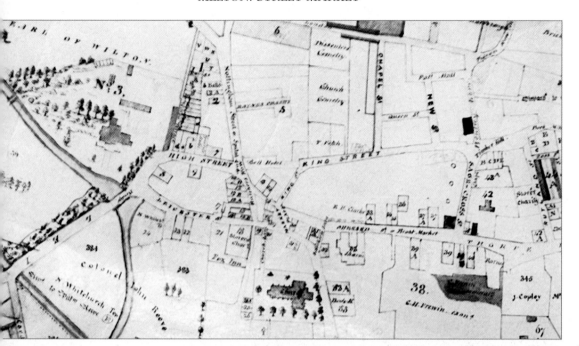

Detail of a map produced in 1871 based on the enclosure awards for Melton Mowbray in 1760. Large open areas are indicated in the centre of the town. Spital End to the Market Place and on to the Beast Market are clearly indicated.

The market on Nottingham Street.

South Parade with the Tuesday market in operation in the middle distance, *c.* 1905.

Sherrard Street, formerly the Beast Market, with the street market in progress, *c.* 1907.

Nottingham Street viewed from the junction of High Street and South Parade, *c.* 1912. Goods are being prepared for sale.

Nottingham Street from the north, *c.* 1905.

A Stilton cheese fair drawing to a close at the end of an auction held in the Market Place, 1904.

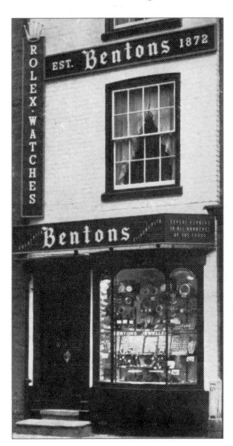

Tuesday market in the square, *c.* 1925.

Benton's shop was situated for many years opposite the Market Place in the town centre.

Market day in Cheapside, 1903. The Stamford & Spalding Bank is in the middle distance and Nottingham Street is beyond.

A twenty-first century view from the junction of High Street and Cheapside into Nottingham Street, showing the Corn Cross, which marks the site of the ancient market where sheep and then grain were sold for hundreds of years.

Sherrard Street, *c*. 1928. In the centre background stands the Carnegie Library. Extensive changes have taken place in the area on the left since this photograph was taken. The street market is held twice weekly on the wide pavement. Moore's Café was demolished as part of a road widening scheme, and the building was eventually replaced by Safeway.

The Market Place from the church tower, 1903.

Saturday street market and the Market Place. St Mary's church is in the background.

The 'Barnes Block' adjacent to the Market Place, *c.* 1910. The building housing Gill Motor Garage was demolished in the 1960s, thus increasing the space for the street market as shown above.

The street market in progress before the 'Barnes Block' was demolished, 1930s.

MELTON: FARMERS' MARKET

Customers purchasing produce at the farmers' market held every Friday on the site of the weekday cattle market.

Pauline Marriott selling her home-grown produce from Goosenest Farm, Wymeswold. The Marriotts raise their own sheep and cattle but their speciality is Gloucester Old Spot pork, which is free range.

Michael Walker from Potters Hill Farm selling cheese made at Long Clawson Dairy. All the milk produced on Michael's farm on the grasslands of Leicestershire is converted into cheese, particularly Stilton.

Satisfied customers at the farmers' market.

Advertisement for the farmers' market.

Steve Brewin from Bisbrooke Ostrich Farm selling fillet steaks. Steve brings a portable grill to market, enabling his customers to sample the splendid cholesterol-free meat from ostriches raised in Rutland.

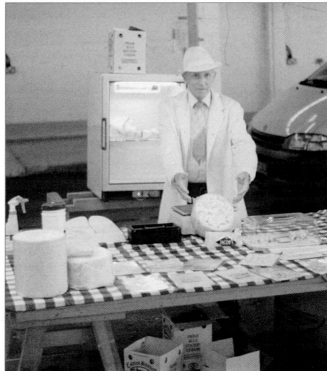

James Stokes, chairman of Colston Bassett and District Dairy Ltd, selling his company's famous Stilton cheese. For information about this Leicestershire foodstuff, consult *The History of Stilton Cheese* (Sutton).

ANTIQUES MARKET

Reproduction of an oil painting of the Tuesday market, printed *c.* 1925. Today this view is a collector's item. Suitably framed it might easily be offered for sale at the antiques market held in the Market Place every Wednesday.

Antiques and collectibles on sale in the Market Place. This picture shows a similar view to the one above but over seventy years on.

A reproduction of the medieval market cross, the Butter Cross, in the Market Place, surrounded by the Wednesday antiques market.

The famous Melton Mowbray street market, 1905. Containers and other objects on view in this photograph could now be resold at the weekly antiques market as collector's items.

ST MARY'S CHURCH

St Mary's viewed from the Play Close, *c.* 1905. Sheep are being held on the grassy field before being conveyed to the cattle market for sale.

Parkland owned by the Town Estate with St Mary's in the background. The church, bandstand and steps to the River Eye can be seen, a view that encouraged visitors to the town before the First World War to enjoy a trip on the river.

Undoubtedly the finest church in Leicestershire: St Mary's in 1910. It was a tourist attraction when this picture was taken and remains well worth visiting.

Interior of St Mary's church, looking from the nave to the chancel, 1903.

St Mary's is high in the background of this photograph of Burton Street taken just after the First World War. This road was a hive of activity and is even more so today, including as it does some interesting shops, public houses and a hotel. An historic thoroughfare to the right of the photograph reveals the sign of The Red Lion. In the escapade infamously known as 'painting the town red', Lord Waterford threw this sign into the Melton to Oakham Canal off Burton Street.

St Mary's church tower from the Bede House garden off Burton Street, 1905.

St Mary's from Burton Street, 1910.

ANNE OF CLEVES

Anne of Cleve's house, 1920s. Originally built as a dwelling for a parson in 1384, it was acquired by Henry VIII during the dissolution of monastic holdings in the mid-sixteenth century. On the advice of Thomas Cromwell the king took Anne of Cleves as his fourth wife, but Henry took an instant dislike to her, calling her his 'great Flanders mare'. He divorced Anne as quickly as possible. However, after Cromwell was beheaded, some of his property was granted to Anne to provide her with an income. It is intriguing to think that she might have visited this house, but in fact there is no evidence that she ever did so, although she certainly received rent from the property. Anne outlived Henry VIII, his son Edward VI and all five of Henry's other wives. She and Princess Elizabeth supported Mary at her coronation. Anne never returned to Cleves but lived at Chelsea Manor until her death in 1557 aged forty-two.

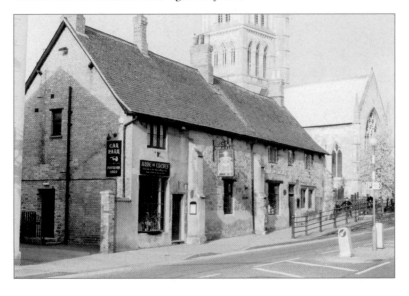

This interesting building, now a public house serving food, is well worth a visit. It was opened as licensed premises by Everard's Brewery in 1995.

CARNEGIE MUSEUM

he Carnegie Library, 1906. Opened in 1905, it was converted to become the town's museum in 1977.

n internationally
nowned exhibit at the
arnegie Museum is a
o-headed calf. It was
elivered near Oakham
the 1890s by the
elton Mowbray
eterinary surgeon
stus Littler, who
actised out of Elgin
odge off Scalford Road.
he lodge was built by
hn Ferneley, the
mous sporting painter.
he calf was once
hibited in the foyer of
e surgery but was
onated to the museum
the 1970s.

Many exhibitions are held at the museum; they attract considerable interest and are always worth visiting. This photograph shows the curator Jenny Dancey in October 2000 checking a display about the Boer War.

tilton cheese has generated considerable interest in and income for Melton Mowbray. It is well represented in the useum. This sign hung in front of Frank Fryer's Stilton cheese dairy at Somerby in the 1930s.

Art exhibitions are strongly supported by Leicestershire County Council's Museums, Arts and Records Service. This photograph was taken in September 1999 and shows a display of illustrations produced by the artist Rigby Graham and held by the museum's trust. Left to right: John Howard, County Councillor and Vice-Chairman of Leicestershire County Council, Pat Lesley representing the Friends of Leicestershire Museums Service, and Rigby Graham.

REGAL CINEMA

Erected in 1933 by local builder Denman's to a design by Riley architects, the Regal opened in King Street on Thursday 25 January 1934. Few changes have been made to the 1930s façade. It was built as an 890-seat cinema, but in 1979 the building was purchased by Zetters who constructed a bingo hall in the stalls area and converted the circle into a smaller cinema.

Advertisement published in the *Melton Times* on Friday 9 February 1945. The adjacent cinema was run jointly with the Regal by the manager A. Scarborough. The Plaza, originally called Melton Picture House, was built and opened in 1920 by Ernest Clarke. It had 800 seats and was renamed the Plaza in 1939. Bingo was introduced at the Plaza in 1960 and eventually became more popular than films, running four nights per week by October 1962. In 1974 the Plaza closed and was demolished.

REGAL CINEMA

Phone 251   Manager: A SCARBOROUGH

FRIDAY & SATURDAY
"HIS BUTLER'S SISTER" (U)
Starring Deanna Durbin, Franchot Tone & Pat O'Brien
Also Good Supporting Programme   The March of Time

Monday, Tuesday & Wednesday. February 12th, 13th, 14th Leslie Howard, Wendy Hiller & Wilfred Lawson Starring in the Re-issue of **"PIGMALLION"** (A) Also Good Supporting Programme including **"CARIBBIAN ROMANCE"** A short film not to be missed	Thursday, Friday & Saturday February 15th, 16th, 17th Maria Montez & Jon Hall in **" ALI BABA AND THE FORTY THIEVES "** With Turham Rey Also Good Supporting Programme

TIMES OF SHOWING
MONDAY TO FRIDAY CONTINUOUS FROM 5-45
SATURDAY CONTINUOUS FROM 2 P.M.
MATINEES TUESDAY & THURSDAY 2 P.M.

PLAZA CINEMA

'Phone 251   Phone 251

FRIDAY & SATURDAY
Basil Rathbone & Nigel Bruce in   " SPIDER WOMAN " (A)
With Gale Sondergaard   (Murder Mystery Melodrama)
Also Alan Jones & June Vincent in "LUCKY DAYS " (U)
With Betty Kean

Monday, Tuesday & Wednesday February 12th, 13th, 14th Maria Montez & Jon Hall in **" ALI BABA AND FORTY THIEVES "** With Turham Rey Also Good Supporting Programme	Thursday, Friday & Saturday February 15th, 16th, 17th Leslie Howard, Wendy Hiller & Wilfred Lawson Starring in the Re-issue of **"PIGMALLION "** (A) Also Grand Supporting Programme including **"CARIBBIAN ROMANCE"**

TIMES OF SHOWING
CONTINUOUS EVERY EVENING FROM 5-45 P.M. SAT. 5-30.

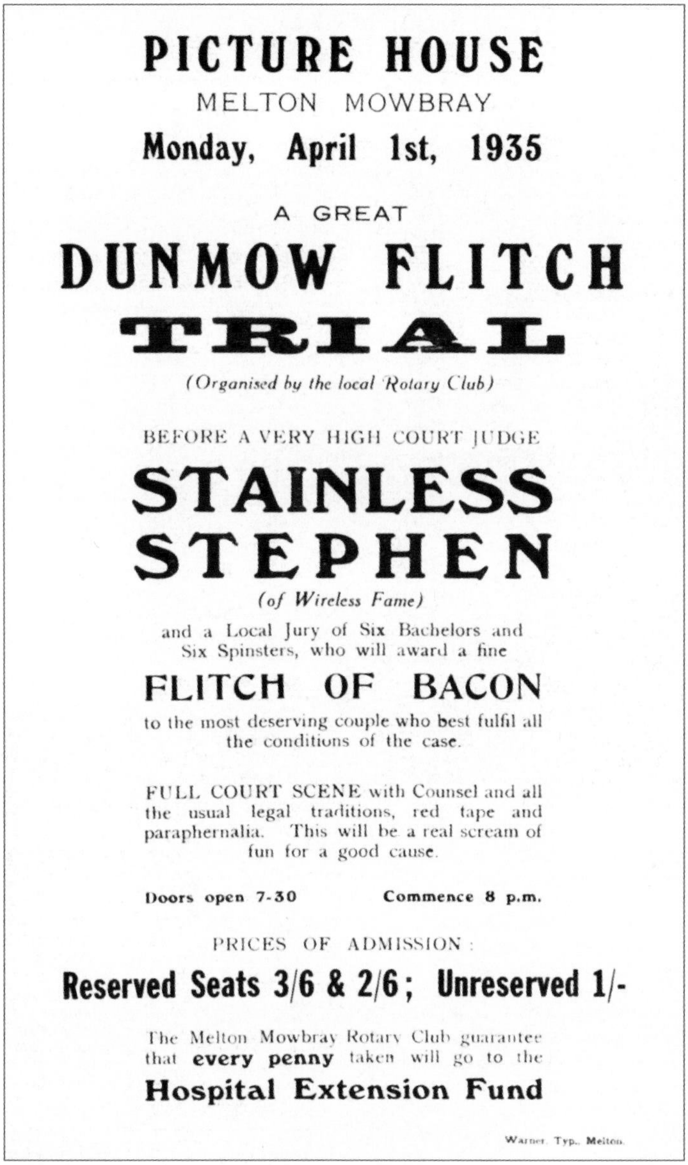

PICTURE HOUSE

MELTON MOWBRAY

Monday, April 1st, 1935

A GREAT

DUNMOW FLITCH
TRIAL

(Organised by the local Rotary Club)

BEFORE A VERY HIGH COURT JUDGE

STAINLESS
STEPHEN

(of Wireless Fame)

and a Local Jury of Six Bachelors and
Six Spinsters, who will award a fine

FLITCH OF BACON

to the most deserving couple who best fulfil all
the conditions of the case.

FULL COURT SCENE with Counsel and all
the usual legal traditions, red tape and
paraphernalia. This will be a real scream of
fun for a good cause.

Doors open 7-30   **Commence 8 p.m.**

PRICES OF ADMISSION :

Reserved Seats 3/6 & 2/6 ; Unreserved 1/-

The Melton Mowbray Rotary Club guarantee
that **every penny** taken will go to the

Hospital Extension Fund

Warner Typ., Melton.

Advertisement for 'A great Dunmow Flitch' (a side of a pig, salted
and cured) to be awarded to the winners of an early 'Mr & Mrs'-
type quiz. This unusual fund-raising function originated in the
village of Little Dunmow in Essex at the Augustinian priory where
the monastic adjudicator awarded a flitch of bacon to any couple
who could give proof that they had spent the first year of married
life in unbroken harmony. In the sixteenth century, after the
dissolution of the priory, a jury of six bachelors and six maidens was
appointed. This idea spread throughout the English countryside and
was certainly taken up by the Melton Mowbray Rotary Club in the
1930s as a way to raise funds. It became a tourist attraction for the
area between 1920 and 1939.

The Regal. This fine old cinema is well worth a trip for visitors and local people alike. Why travel out of the area when all the up-to-date films are available here?

John Merryweather the owner of the Regal, admiring his unique collection of historic films stored on the premises. The earliest reel was taken in 1912 of the Quorn Hunt at Kirby Gate and is stored alongside many other historic records of Melton Mowbray.

2

Melton Borough

Belvoir Castle standing high on the skyline on the escarpment of the Vale of Belvoir. Without doubt this is the leading tourist attraction in the area around Melton Mowbray. Other places of interest in this extremely rural area are hidden in isolated villages. Forward planning is essential if the best of the district is to be enjoyed. Events that take place in the area on a yearly or occasional basis are worth a visit and are recorded in these pages. Explore the countryside and use this book as your guide.

GOLF CLUB

Melton Mowbray Golf Club on the Waltham road leading out of Thorpe Arnold. It was established over seventy years ago. From the eighteenth green you can step straight into the excellent clubhouse.

Visitors are welcome at the club and tourist packages are available. For further information contact the Secretary.

BELVOIR CASTLE

Belvoir Castle, photographed by Townes of Melton Mowbray in 1910. Tourists will be delighted by the quality of the historic displays and the special events held at the castle.

he pre-guardroom walls are lined with nineteenth-ntury muskets. The weapons were commissioned by e fourth Duke of Rutland when he was governor of eland from 1790 to 1800 for use by the icestershire Militia.

The castle guardroom. Straight-bladed swords used by the 21st Light Dragoons are displayed in a circle.

A seventeenth-century Chinese horse standing in the rose garden. It was presented to the fifth duke in 1831 by Admiral Sir Thomas Cochrane who 'obtained' it in China.

The fifth Duke of Rutland.

Statue by Caius Cibber (1630–1700), court sculptor to Charles II.

A display of statues below the rose garden, many by Caius Cibber.

...ll Brittain's bugle: he sounded the call at the Charge ... the Light Brigade at Balaclava but died of his ...ounds on the battlefield. The bugle is displayed in the ...useum dedicated to the 17th/21st Lancers at Belvoir ...astle.

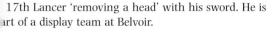

... 17th Lancer 'removing a head' with his sword. He is ...rt of a display team at Belvoir.

...uglers of the 17th Lancers sounding the charge on the ramparts to Belvoir Castle.

The 17th Lancers at a re-enactment display.

Presenting the colours.

Preparing to charge the 17th Lancers at a re-enactment event, Belvoir Castle, May 2000. Below the ramparts of the castle the display team recreated a splendid sequence of nineteenth-century military training manoeuvres including sword play, use of lances in 'tent pegging' and protecting a charge with musket fire.

enry VIII by Holbein. This world-famous painting
as purchased by the fourth Duke of Rutland in
787 and is now on display in the picture gallery at
elvoir.

Belvoir peacocks on the castle lawn. The birds feature
in the coat-of-arms of the Duke of Rutland.

seventeenth-century silver wine cooler. It weighs
,979 ounces and was purchased by the third Duke in
682 for £616 10s.

The dining room with its magnificent ceiling.

A display of medieval jousting is watched from the grass-covered ramparts by tourists. Tournaments usually take place at the castle twice a year.

The red knight and the black knight cross lances to protect the fair lady.

Preparing to 're-charge' in the lists after bein 'unhorsed'.

elvoir Castle's kitchen with
pen range and spit, numerous
ems of everyday utensils from
mes gone by.

elow the kitchen stairs is the entrance to a tunnel
ith a railway wagon inside. This 3 mile railway track
as built in 1815 to convey coal from the Grantham
anal to the castle.

he Marquis of Granby by Sir Joshua Reynolds. The
Marquis was the Commander-in-Chief of the British
rmy at the Battle of Warburg in July 1760. He led the
harge of the British cavalry in this conflict of the Seven
ears War against the French, his bald head glistening
the sun. Hence the phrase 'Going for it bald headed'.

ST MARY THE VIRGIN

The church of St Mary the Virgin, seen from Market Street, Bottesford, 1905. St Mary's is situated in a large village in the Vale of Belvoir. There are good pubs and pleasant walks around the church, which is the final resting place of the Dukes of Rutland.

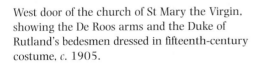

Belvoir Lane with the church of St Mary the Virgin, before the First World War.

West door of the church of St Mary the Virgin, showing the De Roos arms and the Duke of Rutland's bedesmen dressed in fifteenth-century costume, c. 1905.

Part of the chancel of St Mary the Virgin, including the very fine collection of marble monuments to the Dukes of Rutland, 1920s.

Flemmings Bridge, built in 1607 at the expense of Dr Samuel Flemming, rector of St Mary's from 1581 to 1620. It is situated to the south of the church, crosses River Devon and carries a very pleasant village footpath (see page 52, *Leicestershire Memories*, Sutton).

WYMONDHAM WINDMILL

Wymondham Windmill, *c.* 1905. Built in 1813 by Thomas Compton, it was run for many years in the late nineteenth and twentieth centuries by Thomas Oldham and his son.

In April 1987 the property was purchased by William Towndrow. He and his son David began reconstructing the outbuildings and working on the maintenance of the mill. It now has a visitors' centre.

Alterations to the windmill in 1980, when it was owned by William Naylor. The cap was removed and the top of the mill was rebuilt by Nigel Moon, who is standing next to the iron windshaft.

Two views of the windmill showing the restaurant, craft shop and souvenir shop. The open door in the picture on the left leads into the mill. The tower is open to the public free of charge and it is well worth a climb to the top, examining the working system on the way up and enjoying some excellent views from the windows.

During the working life of the windmill, corn was ground here, loaves and pies were baked using pork from animals raised in the extensive piggeries. Melton Mowbray pork pies were a speciality. The original bakehouse stood to the right and the buildings in the centre background were the pigsties. The latter now display farming equipment and include an area for visitors to enjoy light refreshments.

PORK PIE & STILTON TRAIL

Tourism played an important part in generating income for Melton Mowbray from the Victorian period onwards. This unusual postcard, dating from about 1910, was sent from the town to the USA before the First World War. The folded cardboard 'Pork Pie' wallet illustrating the town included twelve small photographs.

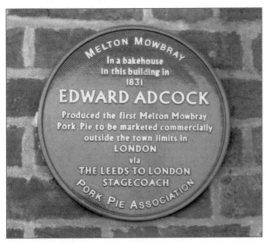

Edward Adcock commercialised the production and marketing of the world famous Melton Mowbray pork pie in 1831 from a bakehouse on Leicester Street. This historic site displays a blue plaque.

Stephen Hallam making the famous hand-raised Melton Mowbray Pork Pie, raising the paste around the dolly.

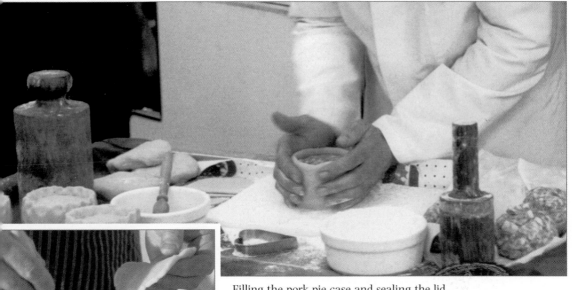

Filling the pork pie case and sealing the lid.

Dickinson and Morris's pork pie bakehouse and sausage shop. This is an essential destination for all tourists interested in the famous Melton Mowbray pork pie. Demonstrations of the methods used to make the famous pork pie can be arranged at the shop.

Joseph Morris standing at the entrance to Dickinson and Morris's café, c. 1920.

Stilton cheese and the Melton Mowbray pork pie should be considered together and on pages 50–55 the author has put together his own Pork Pie and Stilton Trail. The trail begins in the village of Wymondham, seen above in 1977. This building at the junction of Edmondthorpe Road and Main Street is probably one of the oldest surviving centres of cheese-making in England and dates from before 1650. Stilton and other cheeses were manufactured on this site when it was part of a dairy developed in the medieval period. (For further information see *The History of Stilton Cheese* and *The History of the Melton Mowbray Pork Pie*, Sutton.)

Unpressed cream cheese was produced in Wymondham in the 1500s. It developed a blue vein and it was the resulting cheese that almost certainly came to be called Stilton. Peter Hill, owner of Wymondham Dairy, paid for the erection of this monument on the wall of The Bowery on Main Street.

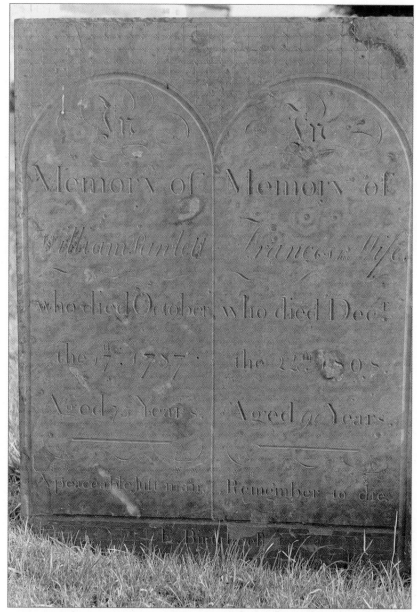

Frances Pawlett (1720–1808) was born in Sproxton to Richard and Dorothy Pick. Her mother, née Thorne, came from nearby Edmondthorpe. The Picks and Thornes were keen farmers and cheese producers. Frances married twice, first to Richard Andrews in 1739. They rented a farm in Wymondham but he died in 1741, and she married William Pawlett of Market Overton in 1742. Frances was a cheese-maker for all her working life, having learned the skills from her mother. With her husband and Cooper Thornhill, the landlord and owner of The Bell Inn at Stilton on the Great North Road, she developed Frances's Stilton cheese. Because of her skills and entrepreneurial ability Stilton became the King of English cheeses. Her gravestone is near the entrance to the main door of Wymondham church.

Tuxford and Tebbutt, the only dairy producing Stilton cheese in Melton Mowbray. The company began making Stilton on this site in 1909. The cheese can be purchased at the farm shop on Thorpe End, a few yards from the Carnegie Museum which has exhibits concerning Stilton cheese and Melton Mowbray pork pies.

The Old Dairy, North Street, Melton Mowbray. This very fine Victorian building was built in the 1880s on the instructions of Thomas Nuttall. Similar brickwork was used by his architect in the construction of farmhouses and property owned by Thomas in Beeby, near Leicester. Nuttall opened the very first factory for the production of Stilton cheese in Beeby in 1875 and by 1896 he was the leading manufacturer, winning prizes throughout the world. He also had factories in Melton Mowbray and Uttoxeter. In 1900 he financed his son John's enterprise to open the Stilton Cheese Dairy in Hartington, Derbyshire, which has just celebrated 100 years of operation.

The Melton Cheeseboard in Bowley Court, Windsor Street, Melton Mowbray. Ann Walker is displaying a cut off a full Stilton cheese.

To trace the history of Stilton cheese and Melton Mowbray Pork pie stay a while in the village of Wymondham. Bed and breakfast facilities are available at The Old Rectory. Much of the building is of seventeenth-century construction and some of it may date from the Middle Ages.

The seventeenth-century dovecote has been incorporated into The Old Rectory building.

The Berkeley Arms, Main Street, Wymondham, well worth a visit for a lunch of Stilton cheese and Melton Mowbray pork pie. Left to right: Joan, Michael and Pam about to enjoy a meal.

BURROUGH HILL

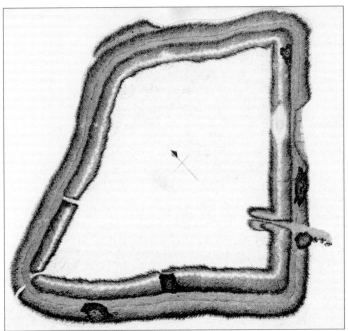

Plan of the Iron Age fort at Burrough Hill, *c.* 600 BC–AD 43. This drawing was produced in 1796 by I. Thailby and remains a fairly accurate delineation of the Burrough Hill Country Park which is open to the public for 365 days of the year.

View from the south, 1920. Sheep are grazing on the escarpment and the Wreake Valley to Melton Mowbray can be seen in the distance.

Sheep grazing on the ramparts of the Jurassic escarpment. A fort and camp were built during the Iron Age on this easily defended hill.

A footpath runs along the top of the surviving ramparts of the encampment's defensive wall.

Visitors flying kites and gliders from the ramparts to the south-west of Burrough Hill camp.

Georgina and Amy at the toposcope. This copper-covered focal point fascinates all visitors who pass on the perimeter footpath.

GATES NURSERIES

Gates Nurseries are laid out in a brick-walled garden built during the reign of 'Farmer George –
George III (1760–1820). This area was once part of the grounds of Cold Overton Hall which
flourished during the Victorian period. The family nursery business on Somerby Road, Cold
Overton, was founded by Frederick Gates over fifty years ago.

Cold Overton Hall, the home of Earl Cowley JP, 1904. It was built during the reign of Queen Anne,
1702–14.

The gated road from Whissendine at Cold Overton, 1905.

An extension in the Victorian garden of Gates Nurseries. The garden centre has an excellent tea room and a children's play area.

Potted plants in the nursery.

Pots for plants.

A display of outdoor plants.

STAPLEFORD PARK

Stapleford Hall, *c.* 1920. The hall is the result of a mixture of building styles dating from about 1500 right through to the turn of the twentieth century. It was purchased in 1986 by Bob Paynton who converted it into a hotel. The house and gardens were first opened to the public in 1953 and quickly developed into one of the finest tourist attractions in the East Midlands.

An engraving of the west front of Stapleford Hall, 1794.

The driveway and main entrance to the hall in 1914 before the demolition of the cottages among the trees.

Medieval cottages in the trees off the driveway at Stapleford Hall. They were demolished by John Gretton in 1914.

Stapleford Hall from the air, 1997.

Greenhouse and garden at Stapleford Hall, *c.* 1920.

unting and shooting deer in Stapleford Park with the hall in the background, *c.* 1830.

ottesmore Hunt leaving Stapleford Hall for the first draw in the Cottage Plantation, February 1937. The Master
Foxhounds was Major C.C. Hilton-Green.

ottesmore Hunt at the lakeside leading to the Cottage Plantation, February 1937.

The old wing at Stapleford Hall, 1937. The grounds were occasionally opened to the public by the Gretton family for fund-raising functions from the 1920s . Then in 1953 the hall and grounds were opened. Attractions eventually included a miniature railway, zoo and a lion reserve. All closed on the death of second Lord Gretton in 1983. The hall is now a hotel and part of the grounds is a golf course.

The gateway, Stapleford Hall, *c.* 1910.

Jane Maxwell with a cub from the lion reserve, 1969. The reserve first opened to visitors in 1968 and was a joint venture with Lord Gretton and circus owner Dick Chipperfield.

Tourists in the lion reserve, 1969.

Philip Maxwell with two lion cubs born at the reserve in 1969.

Jane Maxwell with the peacocks at the zoo aviary, 1969.

The golf course. In the background lie the remains of the Melton to Oakham canal.

Flood control features in the Cottage Plantation, 1998.

Stapleford Hall Country House Hotel from the lake, 1998

hn H. Gretton and the
tapleford Miniature
ailway, 30 August 1998.
fter the hall opened to
ie public in 1953, it was
ecided to expand the
ttractions in the park.
he installation of a 10½
ich miniature passenger
ailway began in 1957 and
was opened by the Earl
f Northesk on 18 May
958. Most of the
ttractions have now been
osed and demolished, but
rtunately the miniature
ailway is opened to the
ublic twice a year.

erkshire, Nickel Plate Road, entering the tunnel,
366.

Mrs John MacConochie, wife of the director of the
Shaw Savill Line, launching a model of SS *Northern
Star* on the lake on 27 June 1963. She is
accompanied by Lord Gretton.

The arrival of SS *Southern Cross*, June 1968. Left to right: H.A. Marshall, Commodore of the *Southern Cross*; Lord Gretton; C.S. Birch, Master of the *Northern Star*.

A pair of swans with their cygnets near the island on the lake.

...ck Pickaver in charge
...aving the tunnel, 1966.

...ssengers entering the tunnel, August 1998.

Models & Miniatures

Stapleford Park nr. Melton Mowbray

**A superb display of
all types of model steam
Road & Rail Vehicles**

Featuring the Stapleford Park
10 1/4 inch Gauge Miniature Railway

Showmans Engine and Fairground Organ

Trade & Craft Stands

Licensed Bar & Catering

Gates Open 10.30am
Admission: £3.00 a car

Caravan & Camping Area
£15 Weekend inc.Admission
(2 Adults & 2 Children)

Supporting LOROS
Leicestershire Organisation for the Relief of Suffering

30th & 31st August 1998

 All Enquiries to: Paul Worbey
Park Farm, Henlow, Beds., SG16 6DF
Tel/Fax: 01462 851711 Mob: 0850 195622

Poster, 1998.

The boat-train awaiting the arrival of SS *Southern Cross* at the side of the lake. In its heyday a trip to Stapleford Park was a memorable experience – a miniature train journey, a trip on a boat, visit the hall, have lunch and then drive around the lion enclosure. In these pages the author has attempted to record a piece of tourist history.

A Shand Mason horse-drawn fire engine, built in 1876 for Sedgwick Brewery, Watford, on display at the Stapleford Country Festival, August 1995.

Models & Miniatures

Stapleford Park nr. Melton Mowbray

By Kind Permission of Lady Gretton

Featuring the Stapleford Miniature Railway

A superb display of all types of model steam Road & Rail Vehicles

27th & 28th August 2000

Supporting LOROS
Leicestershire Organisation for the Relief of Suffering

Advertisement, August 2000.

STAPLEFORD MINIATURE RAILWAY

THIS ECONOMY TICKET IS VALID ONLY ON DAY OF PURCHASE UNTIL THE LAST TRAIN AND MUST BE PRODUCED FOR INSPECTION ON EACH OF THE THREE TRIPS

THIS TICKET IS NOT TRANSFERABLE AND FOR ONE ADULT / CHILD ONLY

PROCEEDS GO TO LOROS

Tickets for the Stapleford miniature railway.

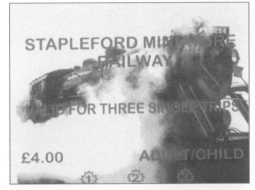

Lady Jennifer Gretton supervising the running of the miniature railway, August 2000.

A train leaving the tunnel, August 2000.

A miniature steam engine negotiating a bend on the way out of Cottage Plantation, August 2000.

The 'plate layer's' cabin.

A steam-driven wagon with a display of miniature steam engines.

A miniature steam engine on display in front of a fairground organ.

The fantastic fairground organ *Wonderland*, a Marengi 98-key powered by a steam engine.

The Melton Mowbray and District Model Engineers' Society, based at Whissendine, with a 5 inch portable track. On the line is working a British Railway Class 10 diesel shunter. In charge of the display is John Lewin, who is overseeing two young customers.

3

Oakham

Should you stay a while in this delightful area of the East Midlands, take the minor roads from Melton Mowbray via Wymondham to Oakham and call at the Black Bull Inn, Market Overton. Enjoy a meal or stay overnight and then examine the medieval stocks on the village green. Proceed to the famous market towns of Rutland and visit the interesting sites and historic villages featured in the following pages.

OAKHAM CASTLE

Oakham Castle, an engraving published in 1769. The drawing is certainly not to scale and this is clear when it is compared with the photograph of the castle below. The remains of the defensive wall still stand and can be seen from the Burley Road car park.

Oakham Castle, c. 1930. All Saints' church is in the background.

The Assizes and Quarter Sessions court in the Norman banqueting hall, *c.* 1920.

Two wreaths placed on display in Oakham Castle. *Left*, to the memory of King Edward VIII, 1910. *Right*, to the memory of King George V, 1936. Both are based on the same horseshoe frame and were created by the people of Oakham as tribute to the two kings.

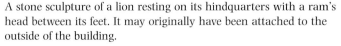

Oakham Castle in need of restoration, 1908.

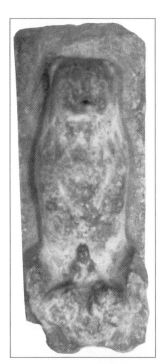

A stone sculpture of a lion resting on its hindquarters with a ram's head between its feet. It may originally have been attached to the outside of the building.

The famous horseshoes in Oakham Castle, featuring Queen Elizabeth II and the Duke of Edinburgh. The origin of the tradition of presenting horseshoes is lost in history but custom demands 'that the first time any peer of this kingdom shall pass through the precincts of his lordship, he shall forfeit as a homage a shoe from the horse whereon he rideth, unless he redeem it with money'. An ornamental shoe takes the place of a plain horseshoe. Queen Elizabeth incorporated a shoe from one of her racehorses in the display.

The Norman banqueting hall with a fine display of ornamental horseshoes.

Advertisement, 2000.

A civil marriage in the Great Hall, Oakham Castle, January 1996.

OAKHAM: FARMERS' MARKET

Oakham Castle and the Friday farmers' market.

Fine cheese and ostrich steaks for sale.

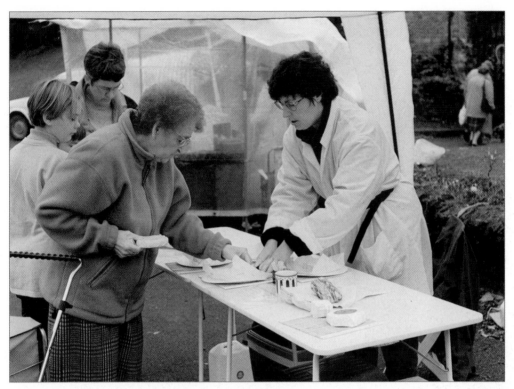

Cath Corbet selling slipcote cheese from Lyddington Dairy.

Brussel sprouts and assorted farm vegetables for sale.

COUNTY MUSEUM

Rutland County Museum, Catmose Street, Oakham. The museum specialises in the farming and rural history of the County of Rutland. Permanent exhibitions feature specific themes and changing exhibitions are installed throughout year. Constructed in 1794, the building became a museum in 1969.

The main hall of the museum building, which was constructed as a home for the Riding School of the Rutland Fencible Cavalry. It was built at the expense of Sir Gerald Noel Bt (1756–1823).

A typical farmhouse dairy laid out as it would have been in the 1930s with butter-making and cheese-production equipment. Slipcote was a cream cheese and at one time was as well known as Stilton. On the display counter are a small cheese mould and a wooden slipcote mould.

An array of cooper's tools, featured with a photographic background of a cooper fitting a rim to a barrel.

Fred Morley's hay wagon, donated to the museum by his family. It was built in Long Clawson and is a fine example of an East Leicestershire cart.

The canal milepost that was originally sited on the towpath of the Melton to Oakham Canal at Turn Overbridge near Ashwell.

A Victorian kitchen, packed with interesting household utensils, many of which are difficult to identify in the twenty-first century, especially for the younger generation.

Ball's milk delivery churn. Edward Ball delivered milk in Oakham at the beginning of the twentieth century and grazed his cows in the grounds of Oakham Castle. This wheeled milk-churn was manufactured by Vipan & Headley who specialised in the production of equipment for dairies throughout the Midlands and beyond. Their main ironmonger's shop was situated on Gallowtree Gate in Leicester. When the family sold the business it was renamed Vipans (1960) Ltd and still operates as an ironmonger in Claymill Road, Leicester.

Engraving published in 1896 when this 'churn on wheels' was patented as a milk-carriage.

A 1920 advertisement detailing Vipan & Headley's equipment.

A horse-drawn rake for gathering hay before carting and stacking.

Lord Lonsdale's game larder. This was built outside his house at Barleythorpe for hanging game birds and animals that had been shot, until they were ready to eat.

Horse-drawn drill for sowing corn on finely tilled soil.

Young visitors viewing the Lord Lonsdale's game larder. The hunters' bag is demonstrated by a selection of stuffed animals and birds – pheasants, partridges, pigeons, snipe, woodcock, hares and rabbits. In 2000 the photographer had the greatest difficulty explaining to these young members of the Grech family (some of them visitors from Malta) why anyone would hang birds and animals, suspend them in such a building and then prepare the matured flesh for cooking and eating. Back row, left to right: Amy, Chloe; front row: Carl, Georgina, James.

A grinding mill constructed in about 1900 for a farm at Normanton. It was sold and set up at Preston, Rutland, in 1921 and ground corn until May 1969. Grain was poured into the chute at the top and fed into the centre of the pair of grindstones. These were rotated by power supplied from the belt of a steam engine. The ground corn passed to the edge of the millstones as flour, falling into a sack suspended on hooks at the front of the machine. Wheat was fine ground into baking flour and barley was roughly ground, primarily as cattle food.

OAKHAM: STREET MARKET

The Market Square, 1909. In 1953 the shops on the right were demolished to make way for the post office. The town pump shelter still stands and offers cover for visitors to the market which is held on Wednesdays and Saturdays. In this photograph the entrance to Oakham Castle is between the shops of Smith and Perkins. All visitors should spend some time at this medieval manor house, especially when the Friday farmers' market is operating in the hall precinct.

End of a day's sale in the market square, c. 1925. On the left, Davis & Sons and Furley & Hasson; on the right, The George Hotel and Whitehouse Sports Outfitters.

A charming view of the market square in the 1920s. The Butter Cross is in the background. The post office now
stands on the right.

Produce for sale in the market square.

The street market, with the Whipper Inn Hotel on the right.

Market square, *c.* 1920, with The George Hotel on the right. Compare this with the view at the top of the page.

The polygonal butter cross with stocks, *c*. 1920. Traditionally, this was the site of Oakham market.

Oakham Wednesday street market still operates alongside the historic butter cross.

CHURCH OF ALL SAINTS

All Saints' is Oakham's parish church. The oldest part of the building is the south doorway which dates from around 1190. Over a 600-year period, changes and additions were made to the structure. The tower and spire were erected during the fourteenth century.

The dedication and unveiling of the War Memorial outside All Saints', 6 April 1922.

The view from the nave to the chancel, All Saints', *c.* 1910.

Church Street with the spire of All Saints' on the right, *c.* 1910.

FEATURES OF OAKHAM

An aerial view of Oakham, *c.* 1920.

High Street looking east, *c.* 1920. Freeman Hardy & Willis Ltd is in the centre background.

High Street looking west, 1905. A coach and pair are on the highway and have just passed Flores House. The picture was taken before the road was widened, disfiguring this historic building which is now the tourist office.

High Street looking east, *c.* 1925.

Mill Street, 1910. A farm cart is passing Hinman's Rutland Motor Cycle Works on the right.

Saturday market in the market square, just visible off the Main Street.

Grainstore Brewery Tap, Station Approach off Station Road. If a visitor to Oakham is interested in fine ale, then a stop at the bar of this brewery is a must. Grainstore Cooking, Triple B, Ten Fifty and other seasonal beers such as Tom Cribb are on offer. The brewery is above the bar in this converted warehouse and it has a visitors' centre.

A thatched cottage on the main street. It was possibly the home of Jeffery Hudson when he retired to Oakham in the seventeenth century.

Blue plaque on the wall of Jeffery Hudson's cottage.

LEICESTERSHIRE CRICKET

Oakham School cricket ground, 7 July 2000. County cricket returned to Oakham after an absence of sixty-two years when Kent played Leicestershire on the Oakham School pitch. The visitors in July 2000 were Surrey.

Many enthusiasts consider the pitch and ground, with their superb facilities, will be an annual venue for a county championship match. Here the flags of Leicestershire and Surrey cricket fly above the splendid pavilion.

Surrey convincingly beat Leicestershire. This is Surrey's Alistair Brown in action; his 215 not out was the highest first class score ever made in Rutland.

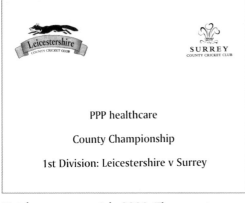

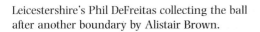

PPP healthcare

County Championship

1st Division: Leicestershire v Surrey

Match programme, July 2000. The organisers say there will be an annual first-class match on this excellent ground.

Leicestershire's Phil DeFreitas collecting the ball after another boundary by Alistair Brown.

4

Rutland

The County of Rutland is a jewel among Midlands shires. This photograph of Normanton church, built in 1826, was taken before 1930. Today it stands on a peninsula at Rutland Water, partially submerged in the lake and surrounded by boulders. It is used in much of the promotional material depicting the county. There is more to Rutland than the reservoir, which covered approximately 3,500 acres when it was created in 1975, but it is difficult to be critical of the twentieth-century civil engineering that made Rutland Water possible. Certainly tourism has increased since the area was flooded. The following pages are an historic account of the county but also incorporate selected modern views of sites that merit a visit.

RUTLAND WATER

Lax Hill near Egleton, just below the Manton to Edith Weston crossroads on the Wing to Hambleton road, 1973. This photograph looks north across rolling countryside and a patchwork of fields.

Early spring, 1976. Rutland Water was filling up and part of the nature reserve was being laid out, with ponds on the left and the site of Lyndon Nature Reserve.

Burley on the Hill beyond the lake in the autumn sunshine, viewed across the lower reaches of the lake with the Upper Hambleton perimeter in the background.

The Lyndon Nature Reserve with Lax Hill behind. Compare this up-to-date photograph with the views opposite, where Lax Hill wood stands high in the background. It is still visible through the trees in front of the Nature Reserve's offices.

The Finch's Arms, Hambleton, offers a splendid view of the lake during lunch. It also provides bed and breakfast accommodation.

Yachting from Whitwell creek.

In 1976 Rigby Graham made a personal artistic record of work on an around Rutland Water. This view shows an earth-moving machine wit Upper Hambleton in the background. It was drawn during th construction of the A606 road from Oakham to Stamfor

The construction of the Barrow Pits, viewed from the southern tip of Hambleton peninsula, looking towar Empingham before the tower conduits were built, 1974.

Harbour Café and Bar off Whitwell Creek. The Whitwell car park is situated near this café. and cycles can be hired nearby – a marvellous way to view the scenery surrounding the lake.

Cottages at Nether Hambleton being demolished in January 1976, recorded by Rigby Graham.

This photograph was taken at the small bridge over the River Gwash by the Hambleton, Whitwell, Edith Weston road junction in 1973. Note the signpost centre right, which indicates the way to Whitwell and Hambleton, and Normanton church in the background.

Spring 1975 and the lake was filling up. Compare this view with the one above.

Normanton church, 1976. 'Operation Landmark' was launched as the water rose and the lower part of the church was filled with hardcore.

Normanton Park by T. Allom, engraved by D. Buckle, *c.* 1820. The church featured above was not erected until 1826. Sir Gilbert Heathcote's Normanton House is in the background; it was demolished in 1925. It is interesting to stand on the high ground off Sykes Lane and compare this picture to the view today.

Constructing the draw-off tower near the dam, summer 1975. This photograph was taken looking towards the Hambleton peninsula and Whitwell, from the Empingham to Normanton road which runs along the south bank.

A view from the dam with the draw-off tower in the background.

The dam from Sykes Lane car park.

RUTLAND BELLE

The *Rutland Belle* off the south bank of Rutland Water. Tickets are available from the pier at Whitwell Creek where the boat is boarded.

Waiting for the *Rutland Belle* at the boarding pier at Normanton church museum.

NORMANTON CHURCH MUSEUM

Normanton church, standing splendid and lonely, 1974. The dam is being constructed in the background.

Normanton Church Museum is well worth visiting. A video presentation records the laying out of the reservoir.

TROUT FISHING

Rutland Water Fishing Lodge tackle shop, restaurant and bar, adjacent to the Normanton car park on the south shore.

Boats lined up for hire by people who want to fish for trout on the lake.

BUTTERFLY FARM

The butterfly farm and aquatic centre near the car park off Sykes Lane on the north bank of Rutland Water.

Swallowtail butterfly. Was the 'Great Tower' by the sculptor Alexander, erected in 1980 on the north shore near the butterfly farm, influenced by the insect's wings? The work of art carries the words 'not intended to be descriptive, so these works do not represent figures or objects'. This fine piece of modern sculpture stands among trees.

YEW TREE AVENUE

The gates to Yew Tree Avenue on the Clipsham to Castle Bytham road, 1922. This avenue of superb topiary is maintained by the Forestry Commission. Originally it was the driveway to Clipsham Hall.

Clipsham Estate Head Forester, Amos Alexander, began trimming these unusual yews in 1870. He lived in this cottage at the gatehouse. Topiary began as a hobby for Amos and the work was continued by his son Charles. During the Second World War the avenue became overgrown but was taken over by the Forestry Commission in 1955.

'A A' – Amos Alexander – the initials of the forester who began trimming these yew trees in 1870.

A Rutland horseshoe.

A yew tree that is over 200 years old.

Windmill.

These beautiful trees are trimmed by the Forestry Commission every September. It endeavours to maintain the original designs.

Peacock and sculptured symbols. Occasionally changes of design do take place on approximately 150 yew trees.

OLIVE BRANCH

The Olive Branch public house, Clipsham, 1920. When visiting Yew Tree Avenue or Clare's Kiln at Pickworth, it is worth visiting two local pubs, this one at Clipsham and the Jackson Stops at Stretton (opposite).

The Olive Branch public house and restaurant.

Enjoy a local beer produced in Oakham by Grainstore.

JACKSON STOPS

Jackson Stops, an historic public house serving fine food (originally The White Horse). For many years before the 1950s this pub was up for sale, but no buyers were interested and its sign fell down. The only thing marking the building was the agent's board and by popular demand the name was retained.

Pam and Frank sitting in the historic 'Barn' before modernisation took place in autumn 2000.

Hidden under a false ceiling in the 'Barn' bar, these inscriptions still survive. During the Second World War servicemen from the nearby aerodromes at Woolfox and Cottesmore consumed considerable quantities of beer and climbed into the roof area, leaving their mark.

PICKWORTH

All Saints' church, Pickworth, *c.* 1905. All Saints' was built in 1821 and stands a short distance from the site of the medieval church. Only a restored medieval arch now stands in a private garden, the original church having been partially destroyed during the Battle of Losecoat Field in 1470.

The peasant poet John Clare worked as a lime burner at Pickworth. In 1966 the author, together with artist Rigby Graham, compiled a book about the ruins at Pickworth and it included the words: 'This book is a collection of prints which resulted from sketches and ideas inspired by Pickworth, its ruins and its associations. It is not complete nor can it ever be. Pickworth is but a fragment and this little book is a series of fragments.' This illustration was drawn in 1965 and shows the cottage occupied by the foreman who supervised the burning of lime to produce cement. Villagers referred to the site as Clare's Kiln and Cottage. The kiln was restored but the remains of the cottage were demolished.

Poet John Clare (1793–1864) helped to construct this lime burning kiln in 1817. John was born at Helpstone a few miles over the border from Rutland in Lincolnshire and became a leading nineteenth-century poet. Visit the memorial at his cottage in Helpstone.

A verse from John Clare's 'Elegy on the Ruins of Pickworth, Rutlandshire' (1818).

'Since first these ruins fell, how chang'd the scene!
What busy, bustling mortals, now unknown,
Have come and gone, as tho' there naught had been,
Since first oblivion call'd the spot her own?

A dramatic illustration by Rigby Graham from *The Pickworth Fragment* (1966). It features the collapsed, flaming lime kiln.

LYDDINGTON BEDE HOUSE

The south view of the Bede House from the churchyard. This almshouse was developed from the medieval bishop's palace in 1602 by the first Earl of Exeter whose seat was at nearby Burghley, Stamford. The original palace was built on the instructions of Bishops Russell and Smith between 1480 and 1514.

The main hall of the Bede House, c. 1930.

Public footpath and entrance to the Bede House.

Carved timber corner in the great chamber, *c.* 1930.

On 26 August 1547 the dissolution of the monastic property was begun on the instructions of Henry VIII. In 1600 Lord Burghley founded the Jesus Hospital on the site for twelve poor men, two women and a warden. The male incumbents had to be aged over thirty, and the female over forty-five. Small, simple living rooms were constructed to benefit from the charity. This photograph of a Lyddington Bede House living room was taken in about 1910.

Lean-to veranda built in 1745 as a walkway.

An almshouse occupant on the veranda, *c.* 1905.

The polygonal watch tower, part of the bishop's palace complex, 1916.

The Old White Hart public house near the Bede Houses. The local slipcote cheese can be sampled here; bed and breakfast is available.

LYDDINGTON DAIRY

An historic wooden slipcote mould no longer in use.

Delivery of milk to the dairy.

Modern slipcote cheese.

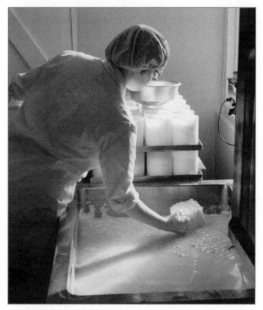

Removing the curd from the vat. The manufacture of this cheese began at about 9.00am and the process was completed by approximately 3.00pm.

Cath Corbet cutting the curd and whey.

A vegetable-based rennet is added to the milk in a vat with a little salt. This coagulates the milk and the curds separate from the whey. The curds are placed in moulds and solidify quickly. This type of cheese should be eaten within two weeks of manufacture. Here cheese is racked in the maturing room.

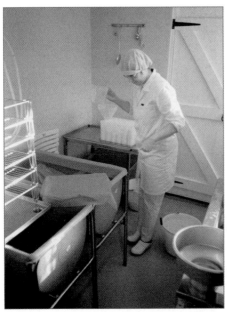

Filling the small moulds with curds to produce miniature cheeses. Lyddington slipcote can be purchased at the local farm market and delicatessen.

Surplus whey being poured into churns for feeding the dairy's pigs. They are also fed on crushed barley and grow quickly into 'porkers' at Cath and Dave Corbet's smallholding.

RUTLAND COUNTY SHOW

Burley-on-the-Hill, *c.* 1905. This is now the home of the Rutland County Show held in May each year. The following six pages feature many interesting activities at the showground.

Pony club competitions in front of the house at Burley-on-the Hill. For many years this was a marvellous site for annual cricket matches.

The smithy, Burley-on-the-Hill. This photograph was taken just after the First World War. The building has been restored and stands on the junction at the Langham crossroads approaching the entrance to the showground.

A pony ready for a competition.

A poster for the 1998
Rutland County Show.

A pony competition in progress.

Cattle being prepared for showing in the assembly area.

A prize-winning bull being displayed with its rosettes and ribbons.

Show jumping.

A competitor taking a fence in the show jumping competition.

Traction engines, ploughs and other historic machinery on display.

Farming implements and machinery on display.

Hot air balloon leaving the showground.

EXTON: STREET MARKET

The Fox and Hounds public house, *c.* 1910. The Fox and Hounds is situated off the village green in Exton, and the green is the home of a market held in May each year to raise money for charities.

Many villages hold street markets but very few can equal the Exton event. This photograph was taken from the village green with the Fox and Hounds public house in the background.

Classic cars on display on the village green in front of the Fox and Hounds, August 2000. This is also an annual event.

Advertisement for this historic public house.

Mary and Sharon in the lounge of the Fox and Hounds.

Top Street and the market square, Exton, *c.* 1910. Where could be a more historic setting for a market than this village, with its medieval heritage and memories of yesteryear?

Tornado Brass performing in the historic market place.

Stamford Road, Exton, *c.* 1930. Compare this historic photograph of the road with the modern view below.

Stamford Road with the street market in full flow.

...xton village green, autumn ...910.

...he green, 2000.

Exton estate barns and the annual village market.

Thatched cottages and visitors to the annual street market.

The villagers open their doors to the public, selling their wares to raise considerable amounts of money for local and national charities.

Selling from the front door to passing visitors and customers.

Fort Henry, Exton, *c.* 1910. It was built as a summerhouse and boathouse in about 1785.

When visiting the village market, make sure you also spend some time at the church of St Peter and St Paul whe
there are internationally recognised monuments. The one on the left of this photograph was taken in 1910 and
dedicated to Baptist Noel, Viscount Campden. It was designed and constructed by Grinling Gibbons in 1686.

WHISSENDINE

Whissendine is an interesting Rutland village. An annual miniature steam train fair is held there along with periodic antique fairs in the village hall adjacent to the White Lion public house, which offers bed and breakfast accommodation.

A view of the village taken from the church tower in 1904 with the White Lion public house in the centre near the Whissendine brook.

Lorna Maybery enjoying a meal in the White Lion's pleasant restaurant.

On the skyline stands Whissendine windmill. In this photograph, taken in about 1900, new sails are being raised.

In 1995 Nigel Moon purchased the windmill and embarked on a major restoration programme. Here the cap is being removed, May 2000.

Nigel grinding wheat to produce flour. He is checking the flow of wheat into the stones. Visits can be organised by special arrangement and eventually the mill will be open on a regular basis.

FEATURES OF UPPINGHAM

Uppingham, *c.* 1905. To the left of centre stands the National School and the Uppingham Improvement Society, demolished in 1974. In the background is the church of St Peter and St Paul.

The post office, market place, Uppingham, *c.* 1910. This small town retains its 'old world' atmosphere and has a collection of interesting small shops.

The market place, Uppingham, 1916. The Vaults public house is in the background.

Victoria building and tower, *c.* 1910.

Printer's Yard off the market square, with its quaint shops and an interesting restaurant.

Main Street, Uppingham, *c.* 1900.

A photograph of the street illustrated above but one hundred years later. There have been few changes to the buildings and some interesting small shops, including especially fascinating secondhand bookshops, are located behind antique façades.

Meedhurst, part of the world-famous Uppingham School, 1925. Meedhurst became part of the educationa foundation when it was purchased and extended by C.R. Haines in 1895.

Brooklands boarding house, c. 1920. Built of brick, in 1861 it became part of the Uppingham School complex and was the home for many Old Scholars.

Stocks of Uppingham, 17 High Street East. William Stocks, a local photographer before the First World War, was one of the leading producers of postcards in the county. He selected a view, captured the scene and two days later was offering copies of his photographs as postcards to customers visiting his shop.

Uppingham, 1905. The photographer stood on the public footpath across the fields, viewing the town from the south-east.

The market place and Falcon Hotel, Uppingham, *c.* 1925. To the left is John Perkins' drapers shop. The post office is to the left of the square with Wilkins & Son tailors and outfitters on the corner.

The famous Falcon Hotel, 1925. This historic coaching inn was run by Adolphe Francis Albert Drake when this picture was taken. Today it is a fine hotel and a good base for enjoying this small, historic town.

ST PETER AND ST PAUL'S

The parish church from the quadrangle at Uppingham School, *c*. 1930.

The church tower viewed from the market square.

St Peter and St Paul's, looking from the nave towards the chancel, *c*. 1910.

UPPINGHAM: STREET MARKET

In 1281 Edward I granted a weekly market on a Wednesday to the Lord of Uppingham and the right to hold a fair for three days in the market square. The market continues to this day, and a fair and cattle sales are held in the market square.

The Vaults public house with the weekly market in progress.

The street market in front of the Falcon Hotel.

High Street West. When visiting the town, be sure to browse through the small, interesting shops along the highway.

The annual Christmas fat stock show held in the market square, Uppingham, 1999.

The entrance to the market square, the site of the Friday street market.

The market square, with its medieval setting, in the twenty-first century.

UPPINGHAM: FARMERS' MARKET

Farmers' market in Mercers Yard, a thoroughfare that runs between the Falcon Hotel and the Uppingham bookshop. Cath Corbet is selling her slipcote cheese in front of the sixteenth-century building. The rear window of an early gabled stairwell is behind her.

FARMERS MARKET DATES

Mercers Yard, Uppingham
2nd Friday of every month 9am-2pm
November 10th
December 8th
December 14th - late night Xmas shopping

~~~~

Oakham - 4th Friday of every month
November 24th - Castle Grounds,
December 12th - Late night (Maltings)
December 22nd - Castle grounds

Free range poultry & eggs, ostrich, pork, beef, lamb, venison, cheeses, honey, vegetables, ice cream & yoghurt, apples & juice, herbs & perennials

Advertisement for the farmers' market.

Bassingthorpe best English beef for sale fresh from the farm.

GOLDMARK'S

Visit Uppingham's Orange Street and find Goldmark's bookshop and gallery. You will be greeted with good humour and offered a cup of coffee. Browse through the vast selection of new and secondhand books, but above all enjoy a walk around the gallery.

Goldmark's is considered by many experts on modern art to be the finest gallery outside London. Examples o work on sale there are featured on the following three pages.

Rigby Graham, *Kalkara and Fort Riccasoli Fort Elmo, Malta*, 1997, watercolour 15 × 21 inches.

Rigby Graham, *Snibston*, 1999, watercolour 15¼ × 22½ inches.

Olive Wooton, *Watersprite and Turtle*, bronze, edition of nine.

Olive Wooton, *Minotaur, Crouching*, bronze, edition o nine.

Rigby Graham, *Owls at Leppits Hill*, woodcut, edition of fifty, three colours 18 × 15 inches.

Barry Burman, *House Beautiful, Pilgrims Progress*, 1998, mixed media, 8 × 7 inches.

George Large, *Staithes*, 1998, watercolour, 18 × 27 inches.

George Large, *York*, 1998, watercolour, 16 × 24 inches.

BIBLIOGRAPHY

Brooke, C., and Sutherland, F. (eds), *Excellence through Independence*, 1999
Brownlow, J., *Melton Mowbray, Queen of the Shires*, 1988
Bryant, A., *1000 Years of British Monarchy*, 1973
Burkett, M., *Kidnapping at Belvoir Castle*, 1998
Clayton, C., *Foxhunting in Paradise*, 1993
Eller, R., *The History of Belvoir Castle*, 1841
Encyclopaedia Britannica, 1951
Evans, J (ed.), *Good Beer Guide*, 1998
Fox, H.S.A (ed.), *Seasonal Settlement*, 1996
Fraser, A., *The Six Wives of Henry VIII*, 1996
Graham, R., *The Pickworth Fragment*, 1966
Gretton, J., *Stapleford Park, Melton Mowbray*, 1958
Hornsey, B., *Ninety Years of Cinema in Rutland and Melton Mowbray*, 1994
Hunt, P.E., *The Story of Melton Mowbray*, 1957
Jenkins, A., *Rutland: A Portrait of Old Postcards*, 1993
Kelly's Directory Leicestershire and Rutland, 1900, 1904, 1916, 1925
Matthews, B., *By God's Grace*, 1984
Matthews, B., *The Book of Rutland*, 1978
McK. Clough, T.H., *The Horseshoes of Rutland*, 1999
Moon, N., *The Windmills of Leicestershire and Rutland*, 1981
Page, W. (ed.), *The Victoria History of the Counties of England: A History of Rutland*, vols I and II, 1975
Penniston-Taylor, R., *A History of Wymondham: Leicestershire*, 1996
Smith, P., *Whissendine, a Rutland Village*, 2000
Woodfield, C. and P., *Lyddington Bede House*, 1988

Uppingham station, 190? It opened in 1894 on a branch line from the London & North Western Railway which was closed in 1964. In the line's heyday students from the public school, visitors and tourists used this railway station. Modern commuters and visitors would consider such a stop a Godsend in the twenty-first century.

ACKNOWLEDGEMENTS

For a number of years the author has considered the idea of producing a book of local history that could also be of interest to visitors to this area of the East Midlands. Help has been provided by a number of people and organisations. The author's grateful thanks are extended to: Rutland County Museum, Tim McK. Clough, Karen Wilson, Melton Mowbray Building Society, Nick Rooney, Frank Piguillem, Cath Corbet, Mike Goldmark, *The Rutland Times*, Mrs D.M. Green, Melton Borough Council, Matthew O'Callaghan, Mark Bowen, Carnegie Museum, Jenny Dancey, Rigby Graham, Tim Williams, *The Melton Times*, Alan Newton, Nigel Moon, Lady Jennifer Gretton, John Wright, Sid Allsopp, The Comptroller, Belvoir Castle. Many of the historic images in the book are out of copyright or the photograph belongs to the author. Where copyright has been retained permission has been granted. Should the author be unaware of the infringement of copyright, he offers his sincere apologies and will make an immediate apology. The author offers his grateful thanks to Pat Peters for processing the manuscript and his publishers for accepting this compilation for publishing.

In 1794 Sir Gerald Noel Bt (1756–1823) raised the Rutland Fencible Cavalry. In 1804 he commissioned the building of this park gun to be used by the local military volunteers. This photograph was taken in about 1905 at the lake at Fort Henry, Exton. Was the weapon filled with shot to take the place of a punt gun for shooting several duck in one go? A model of this gun is on display in the Rutland County Museum.

SELECTIVE INDEX

Adcock, Edward 50
Anne of Cleves 30
Antiques 13, 25
Assize 79

Bede House 29, 122, 123, 124
Belvoir Castle 8, 37, 39, 40, 43
Berkeley Arms 55
Brooklands 146
Burley-on-the-Hill 105, 127, 128
Burrough Hill 56
Burton Street 29
Butter Cross 26, 94
Butterfly Farm 114

Castle, Oakham 78
Catmose Street 84
Cheapside 9, 19
Church Street 96
Churches:
    All Saints', Oakham 95
    St Mary the Virgin, Bottesford 46, 47
    St Mary's, Melton Mowbray 27
    St Peter and St Paul, Exton 149
    Uppingham 147
Cinemas:
    Plaza 34
    Regal 34, 36
Clare, John 121
Clipsham 115, 118
Cold Overton Hall 59
Corn Cross 9, 19
County show, Rutland 127, 129

Dickinson and Morris 51
Dove cote 55
Dunmow Flitch 35

Empingham 106
Escarpment 57

Falcon Hotel 148, 151
Farmers' markets:
    Melton 22, 23
    Oakham 82
    Uppingham 153
Features
    Oakham 97

Uppingham 153
Flores House 98
Forestry Commission 115, 117
Fort Henry 140, 159
Fox and Hounds 133, 134

Gates Nursery 59
Gibbons, Grinling 140
Gloucester Old Spot 22
Goldmark's 153
Golf Club 38
Grainstore 100, 118
Gretton, John 63, 69

Hambleton 105, 106, 108, 110
Helpstone 121
Henry VIII 30, 43, 123
Horseshoe(s) 79, 80, 81, 116
Hunts:
    Cottesmore 65
    Quorn 36

Jackson Stops 119

Lancers 17th 41, 42
Lax Hill 104, 105
Leicestershire Cricket 101
Littler, Justus 31
Lord Lonsdale 88, 89
Lyddington Bedehouse 122

Market places 15, 18, 20, 21, 25
Markets:
    Beast 15, 16
    Cattle 9, 10, 12
    Friday 152
    Pigs 11
    Poultry 14
    Saturday 99
    Tuesday 18
    Wednesday 94
Museums:
    British 7
    Carnegie 31
    Normanton Church 108, 109, 112
    Rutland County 84

Nether Hambleton 106, 107

Nottingham Street 9, 15, 17, 19
Nuttall, Thomas 54

Oakham 77
Oakham School 101
Olive Branch 118
Ostrich 24, 82

Painting the Town Red 29
Pawlett, Frances 53
Pickworth 120
Pork Pies 8, 50, 51

Rutland 103
Rutland Belle 111
Rutland Water 104

Scalford Road 9, 10, 11, 12, 13, 22
Sherrard Street 16, 20
Slipcote 83, 85, 125, 126, 153
South Parade 16
Spital End 15
Stapleford Hall 64, 68
Stapleford Park 62, 65
Stilton Cheese 8, 18, 23, 24, 34, 50, 52, 53, 54, 55
Stocks 94, 147
Street markets:
    Exton 133
    Melton 15
    Oakham 91
    Uppingham 150
Stretton 119
Sykes Lane 109, 110

Thomas Cook 6
Toposcope 58
Tourists 6
Town Estate 27
Trout Fishing 113
Tuxford and Tebbut 54

Vaults 144, 150

Windmills:
    Whissendine 142
    Wymondham 48

Yew Tree Avenue 115, 116